Sunshine for the Soul

Jessica Jean Garrison

Copyright 2016 by Jessica Jean Garrison
Published by Bush Publishing & Associates
ISBN: 978-1-944566-13-5
All rights reserved.

This book belongs to:

_____

Dedicated to my
two daughters
and my son

Let the sun touch your soul

Soak in the love
all around you

Beauty is measured
by the love you give

An ounce of *sunshine* to the soul is like love to an aching heart

Smile, you never know who is looking

Let your smile radiate like the *sun*

Let your love penetrate the hearts of others, like a warm sunny day

A smile a day, keeps joy along the way

Blue skies span the world, as love spans the hearts of the world's desire

Breathe in the beauty all around you

One ray of *sunlight* can bring joy unto the soul

When your soul is nourished, your body is nourished

Positive beats of a heart, pump blood into your soul and life

Sparkle like the *sun*, even if no one sees you

Sing out loud beneath the sunny skies and watch your soul dance

Dance every day,
and allow your soul
to sparkle and shine
like the Sun

When life seems gloomy, shine like the Sun

If we all looked to the ☀ and the warmth and happiness it brings, we could see a way to touch the lives of those around us

Always give
love a chance to
shine

When the world seems dark, add some *sunshine* to your soul

Life without the *Sun* is like a soul without life, both are dark and full of gloom. *Shine* for all to see

When in doubt.....
shine like
the Sun

When in doubt.....
sparkle like a ray of
sunlight

When happiness seems far from you, gaze at the beauty around you, and allow that beauty to soak into your soul, like the *sunshine* seeps into your soul

When your soul seems
troubled, soak in the
sunshine of life,
enjoy the little things
that bring joy

Funny thing....when you focus on joy, it just shows up

Being lighthearted is just that: being light within your heart

The light of the world,
let it shine so deeply
within your heart

Let your own light shine just like the *sun*

We all are unique, shine as you! No one is better at it than your own special self

You were made to shine like the *sun*

You were made to
smile like a warm,
sunny day

Focus on the good
you can do in
the world

Focus on the rays of *sunlight* you can bring to others who may need it

You were made for a special reason only you can fulfill

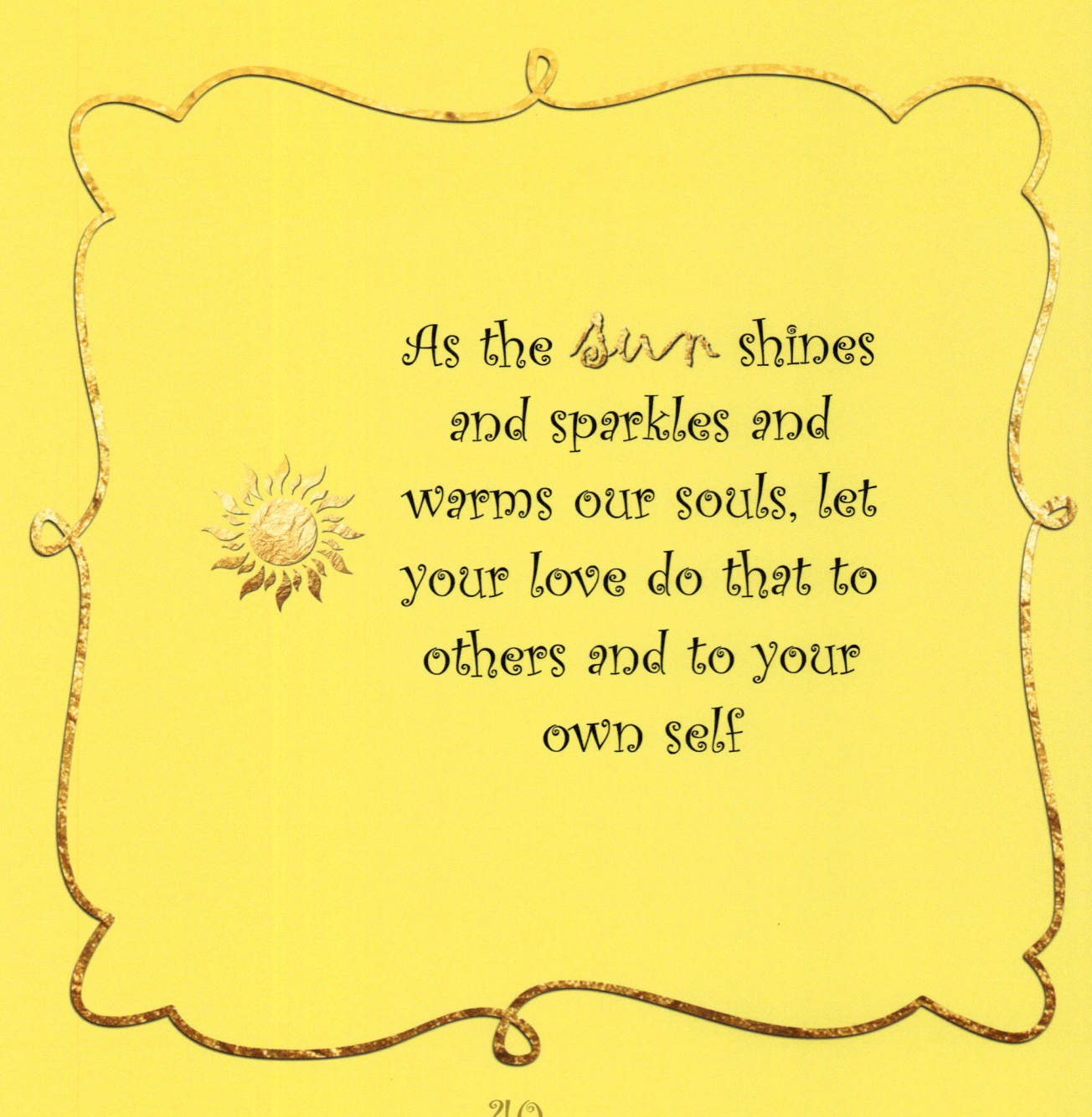

As the Sun shines and sparkles and warms our souls, let your love do that to others and to your own self

Let love soar and reach the bluest of skies

Just the warmth of the *sunshine* brings joy to your soul

Just as the sun
warms a cold day,
an act of love warms
the heart

A sprinkle of sunshine will brighten anyone's day

A warm smile to the heart is like the warmth of sunshine on a cold winter's day. Both provide warmth to the soul

A cheerful giver is like a ray of *sunshine*

Love warms the heart as the Sun warms the soul

When in doubt, smile and laugh, it will create instant *sunshine* in your day

Even if it's gloomy outside, your soul can still create *sunshine*

Dance like nobody's looking and see a ray of light appear in your soul

Let your inner self shine like the *Sun*

Happiness is *sunshine* every day

Loving others will bring *sunshine* your way

When you are a ray of light, people will take notice! So go ahead and *shine*

Let the *sunshine* radiate to the core of your soul and you will get energized with life

Shimmer, sparkle, and shine like the sun for all to see

An act of kindness is *sunshine* to your soul

Sunshine is like joy to your soul

Sunshine warms your heart and soul

Let sunshine seep into your soul, and you will be surprised by the energy you feel

Live, laugh, and love *sunshine* for the soul days

Joy and laughter are sunshine from the inside out

One ray of *sunshine* can brighten a room, as a gentle smile can brighten one's spirit

Always allow yourself to radiate like the Sun

About the Author

Jessica Jean Garrison resides in Oklahoma with her two beautiful daughters and her handsome son. Jessica is a registered and licensed dietitian, a graduate of Oklahoma State University; however, her love of writing sparked her creativity and ambition to nourish adults, as well as young children, with that of beautiful, inspirational books filled with love and joy. Jessica hopes to inspire others to love and enjoy life! May some rays of sunshine fill your soul through her inspirational book, *Sunshine for the Soul*. Jessica hopes that a few rays of light may bring joy and love into your life and bring happiness to your day. Happy soul days!

Printed by Libri Plureos GmbH in Hamburg, Germany